GEOMETRI FOR FUN!

DEVELOP YOUR IMAGINATION

Homeschooling Workbook
for kids 5-8 years old.
Fun and interesting tasks,
exciting activities and
coloring page, that
introduce you an
amazing world
of Geometry.

2D SHAPES

TABLE OF CONTENTS

INTRODUCTION TO THE SHAPES

$2+2=4$

Let's start to learn geometric shapes. Are you ready?

GETTING TO KNOW THE SHAPES

Which shapes do you know? Look on these shapes
carefully and try to remember each one.
By the way, you can color them.

SQUARE   **CIRCLE**   **TRIANGLE**

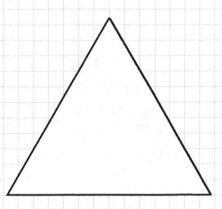

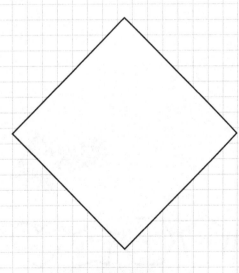   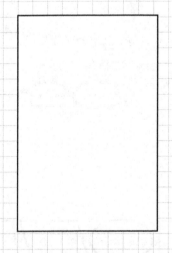   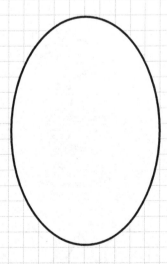

DIAMOND   **RECTANGLE**   **OVAL**

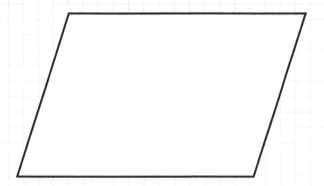

PARALLELOGRAM

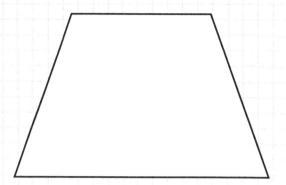

TRAPEZOID

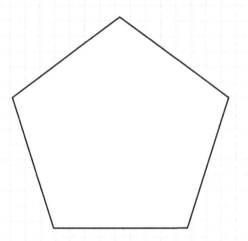

PENTAGON

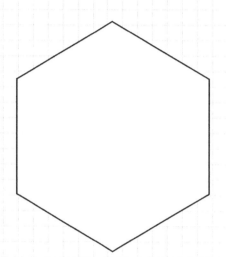

HEXAGON

STAR

HEART

LET'S CHECK!

Let's check how well you remember the shapes. Name each shape, write the name in the next field, and draw your own shape near them.

Circle

GEOMETRY FOR FUN!

WELL DONE! NOW YOU KNOW THE DIFFERENT SHAPES. I HOPE YOU REMEMBER THEM VERY WELL. SO, IT'S TIME TO KNOW ABOUT MORE SHAPES. ARE YOU READY? LET'S GO!

PROPERTIES OF THE SHAPES

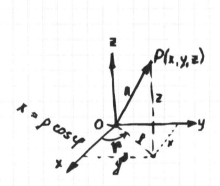

Properties of different shapes, fun tasks, coloring, and exciting activities!

SQUARE

Trace the big square and color the other squares.

Side

Side

Corner

Count all the sides of this shape. Write your result here _____

Count all the corners of this shape. Write your answer here _____

Draw your own squares here as you want..

Choose only the squares from all the shapes and color them in different colors.

How many times is each shape used? Write your answer below.

Find the squares and color them with brown color.

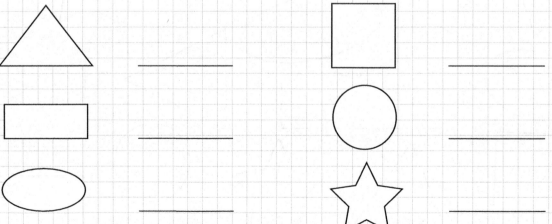

COLOR THE SHAPES

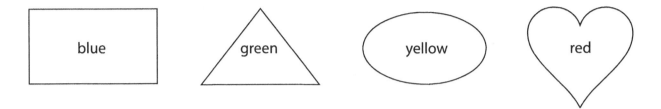

Color the rectangles blue, the triangles green, the ovals yellow, and the hearts red.

WELL DONE!
YOU KNOW ONE MORE SHAPE NOW AND CAN TAKE A LITTLE BREAK AND PLAY.

Color 3 squares pink and the rest orange.

How many squares are there?

☐ **+** ☐ **=** ☐

Pink   Orange   Squares

COLOR THE OBJECT(S) GREEN THAT ROLL

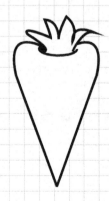
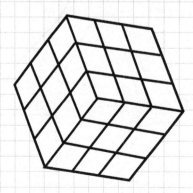
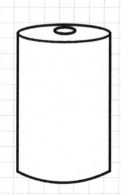

Cut out of paper and assemble the cube

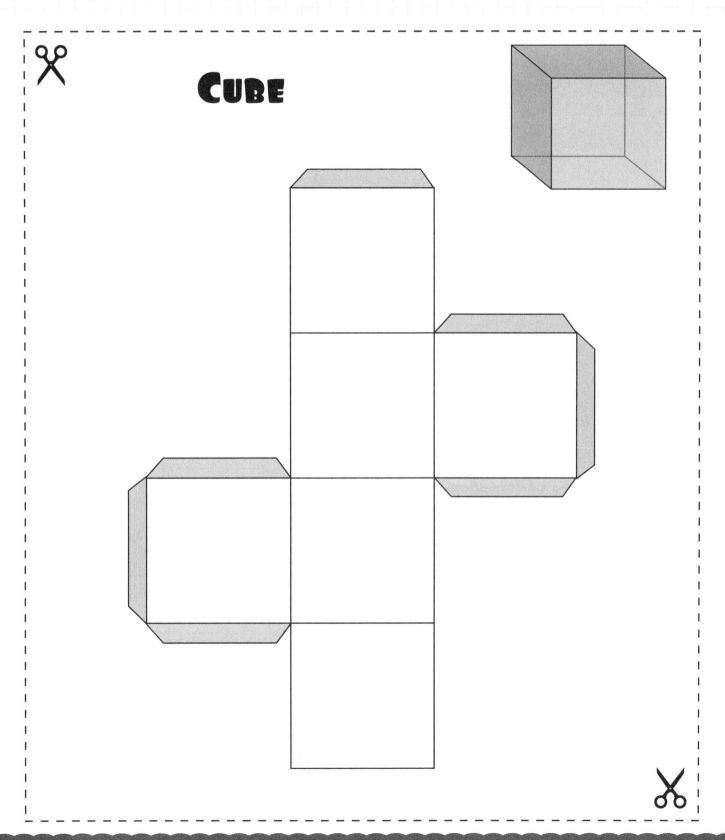

CUBE

CIRCLE

Trace the big circle and color the other circles.

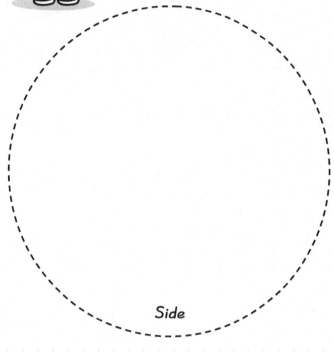

Side

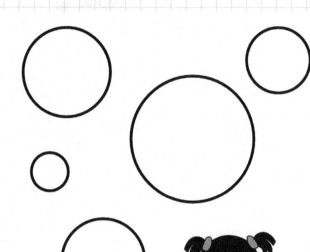

Count all the sides of this shape. Write your result here _____

Count all the corners of this shape. Write your answer here _____

Draw your own circles here as you want...

Choose only the circles from all the shapes and color them in different colors.

How many times is each shape used? Write your answer below.

Find the circles, and color the big circles in black and small ones in silver.

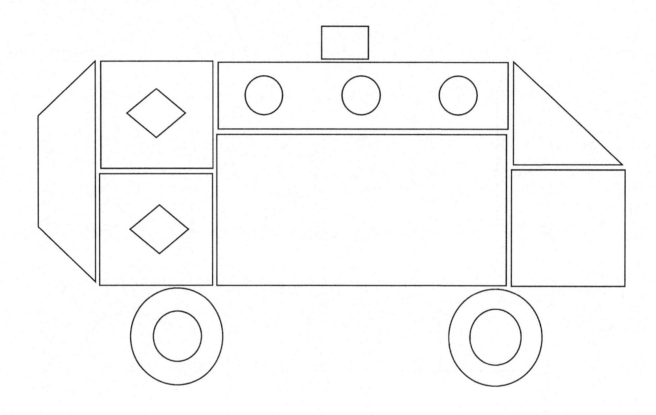

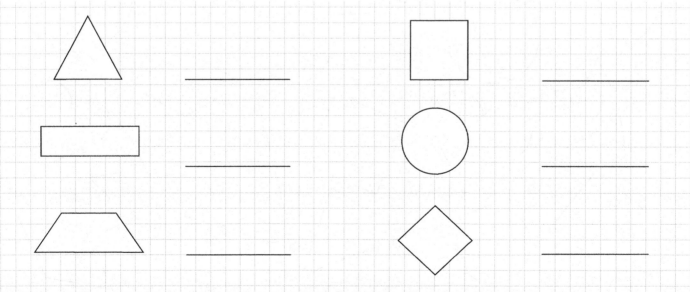

COLOR THE SHAPES

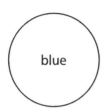 green

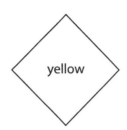 blue

 yellow

brown

Color the squares green, the circles blue, the diamonds yellow, and the stars brown.

WELL DONE!
YOU KNOW ONE MORE SHAPE NOW AND CAN TAKE A LITTLE BREAK AND PLAY.

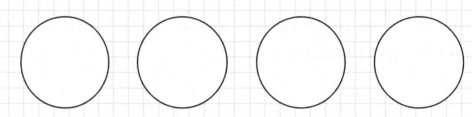

Color 1 circle violet and the rest red.
How many circles are there?

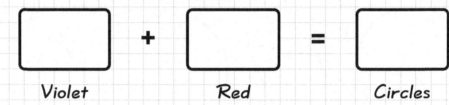

Violet + Red = Circles

COLOR THE OBJECT(S) RED THAT SLIDE

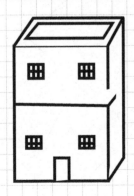

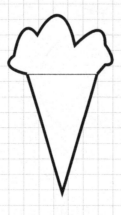

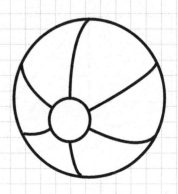

Help the mouse to get back home...

TRIANGLE

Trace the big triangle and color the other triangles.

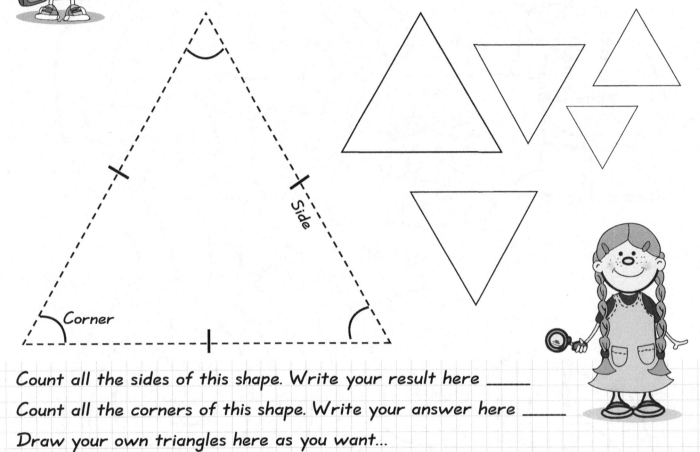

Side

Corner

Count all the sides of this shape. Write your result here _____

Count all the corners of this shape. Write your answer here _____

Draw your own triangles here as you want...

Choose only the triangles from all other shapes and color them in different colors.

How many times is each shape used? Write your answer below.

Find the triangles and color them in the same color.

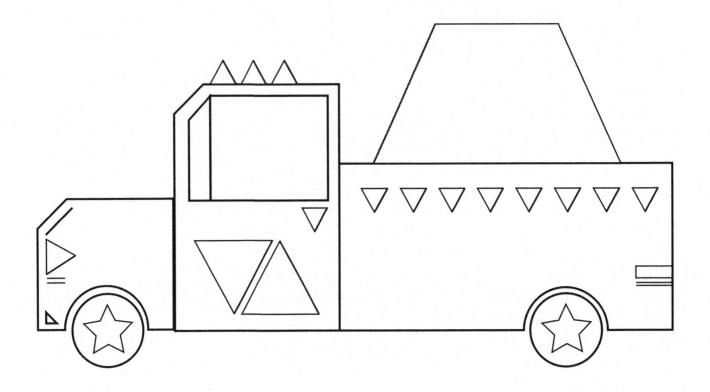

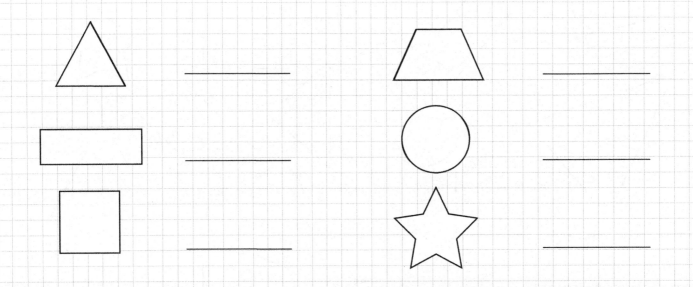

COLOR THE SHAPES

Green Pink Yellow Blue Red Brown

Color the squares green, the triangles pink, the diamonds yellow, the parallelograms blue, the trapezoids red, and the kites brown.

WELL DONE!
YOU KNOW ONE MORE SHAPE NOW AND CAN TAKE A LITTLE BREAK AND PLAY.

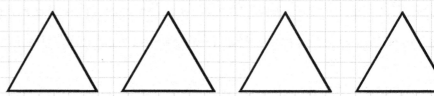

Color 3 triangles pink and the rest orange.

How many triangles are there?

Pink   Orange   Triangles

COLOR THE OBJECT(S) YELLOW THAT STACK

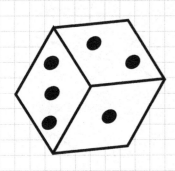

Cut out the paper and assemble the triangular pyramid.

TRIANGULAR PYRAMID

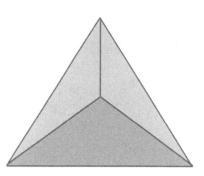

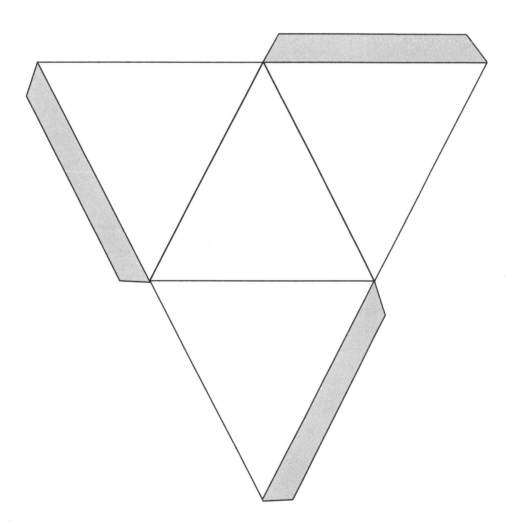

DIAMOND

Trace the big diamond and color the other diamonds.

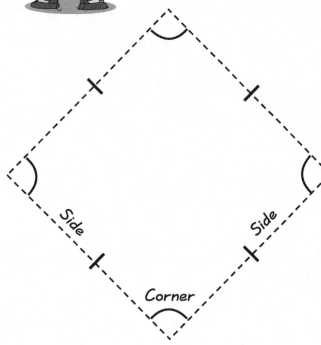

Side   Side

Corner

Count all the sides of this shape. Write your result here _____

Count all the corners of this shape. Write your answer here _____

Draw your own diamonds here as you want...

Choose only the diamonds from all other shapes and color them in different colors.

How many times is each shape used? Write your answer below.

Find the diamonds and color them in blue.

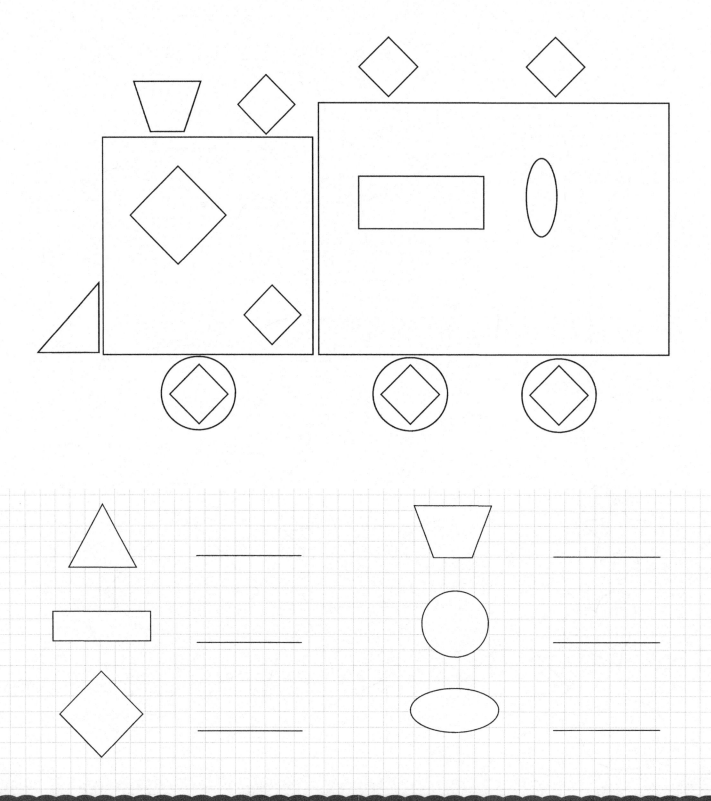

COLOR THE SHAPES

 yellow

 green

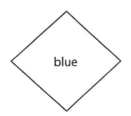 blue

 brown

Color the squares yellow, the circles green, the diamonds blue, and the stars brown.

WELL DONE!
YOU KNOW ONE MORE SHAPE NOW AND CAN TAKE A LITTLE BREAK AND PLAY.

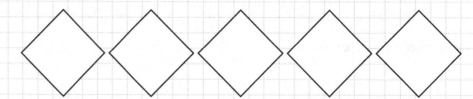

Color one diamond yellow and the rest brown.
How many diamonds are there?

 + 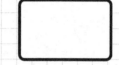 =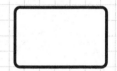

Yellow   Brown   Diamonds

COLOR THE OBJECT(S) ORANGE THAT ROLL AND SLIDE.

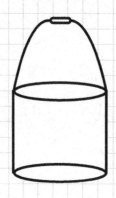

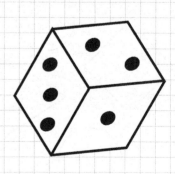

How many apples can you find in this picture? Color as many apples as you want.

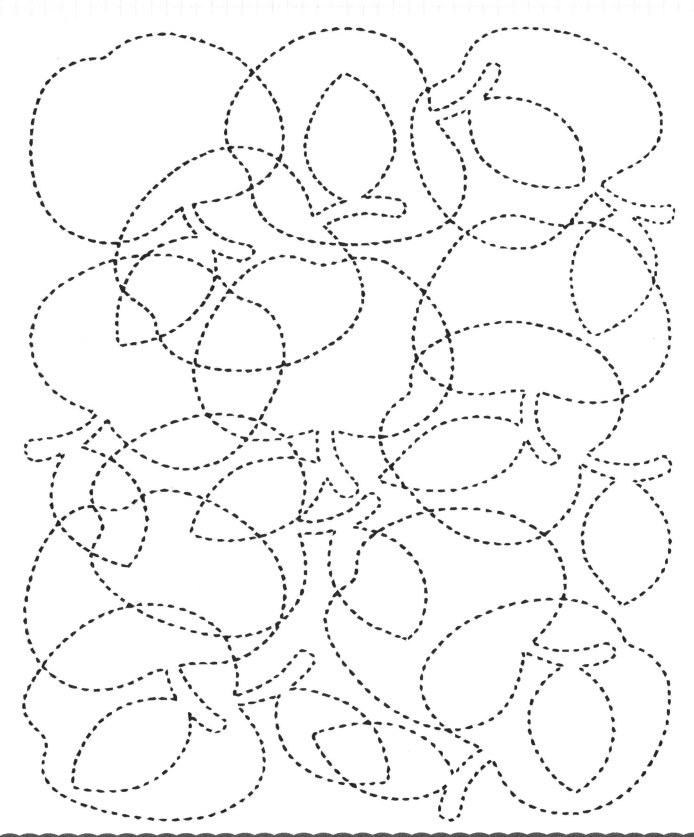

RECTANGLE

Trace the biggest rectangle and color the other rectangles.

Side

Side

Corner

Count all the sides of this shape. Write your result here _____

Count all the corners of this shape. Write your answer here _____

Draw your own rectangles here as you want...

Choose only the rectangles from all other shapes and color them in different colors.

How many times is each shape used? Write your answer below.

Find the rectangles and color them in blue and brown.

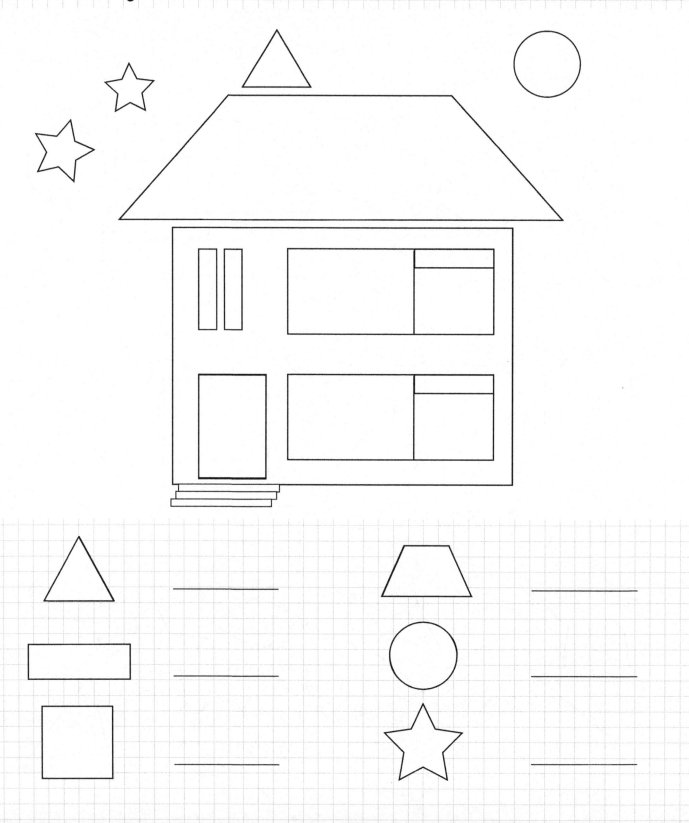

COLOR THE SHAPES

| Pink | Green | Yellow | Blue | Red | Brown |

Color the squares pink, the rectangles green, the diamonds yellow, the parallelograms blue, the trapezoids red, and the kites brown.

WELL DONE!
YOU KNOW ONE MORE SHAPE NOW AND CAN TAKE A LITTLE BREAK AND PLAY.

Color 2 rectangles red and the rest green.
How many rectangles are there?

[ ] **+** [ ] **=** [ ]

Red   Green   Rectangles

COLOR THE OBJECT(S) BROWN THAT SLIDE AND STACK.

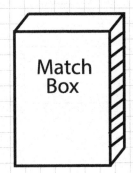

Match Box

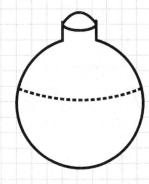

The one who will be held to the star, he is the real King!

OVAL

Trace the big oval and color all other ovals.

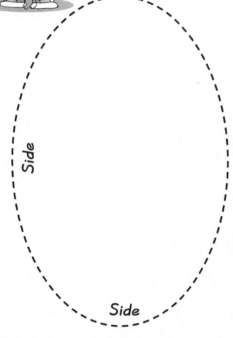

Side

Side

Count all the sides of this shape. Write your result here _____

Count all the corners of this shape. Write your answer here _____

Draw your own ovals here as you want...

Choose only the ovals from all other shapes and color them in different colors.

How many times is each shape used? Write your answer below. Find the ovals and color them in blue. And for the rest of the shapes, color them as you want.

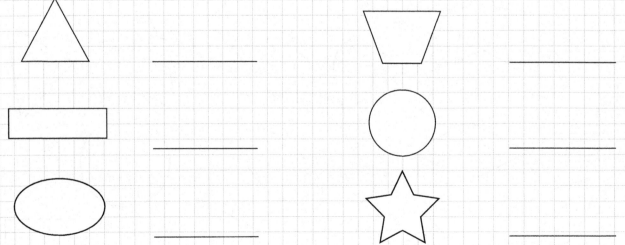

COLOR THE SHAPES

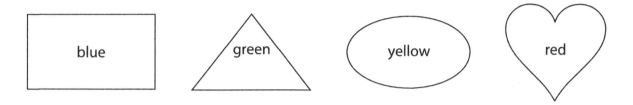

blue   green   yellow   red

Color the rectangles blue, the triangles green, the ovals yellow, and the hearts red.

WELL DONE!
YOU KNOW ONE MORE SHAPE NOW AND CAN TAKE A LITTLE BREAK AND PLAY.

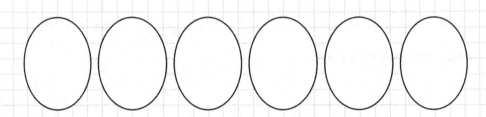

Color 2 ovals blue, 1 oval green, and the rest yellow. How many ovals are there?

	+		+		=	
Blue		Green		Yellow		Ovals

COLOR THE OBJECT(S) RED THAT STACK

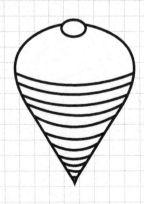

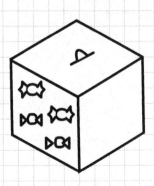

Find out the order of letters and guess the hidden word.

PARALLELOGRAM

Trace the big parallelogram and color the other figures.

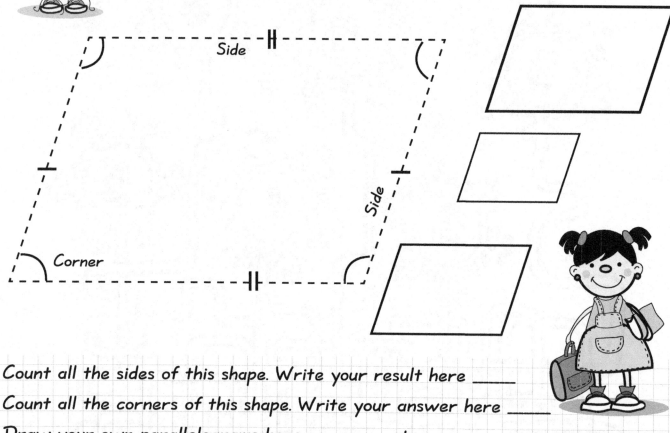

Side

Side

Corner

Count all the sides of this shape. Write your result here _____

Count all the corners of this shape. Write your answer here _____

Draw your own parallelograms here as you want...

Choose only the parallelograms from all the shapes and color them in different colors.

How many times is each shape used? Write your answer below.

Find the parallelograms and color them in the same color.

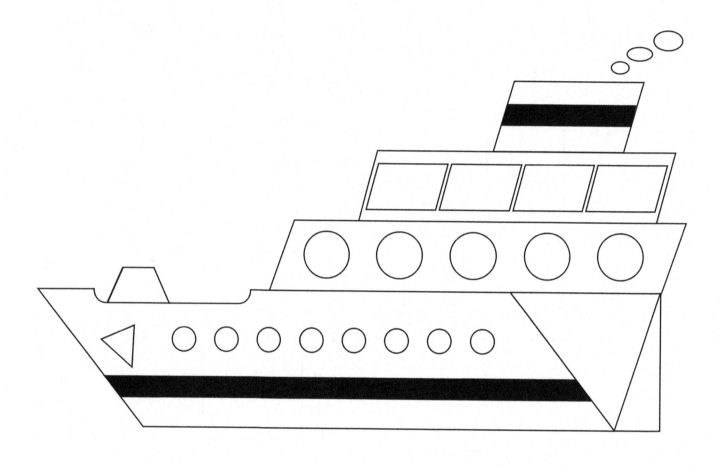

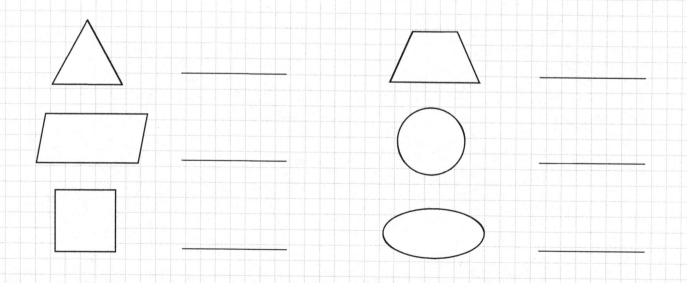

COLOR THE SHAPES

Green **Blue** **Yellow** **Brown**

Color the parallelograms green, the trapezoids blue, the pentagons yellow, and the hexagons brown.

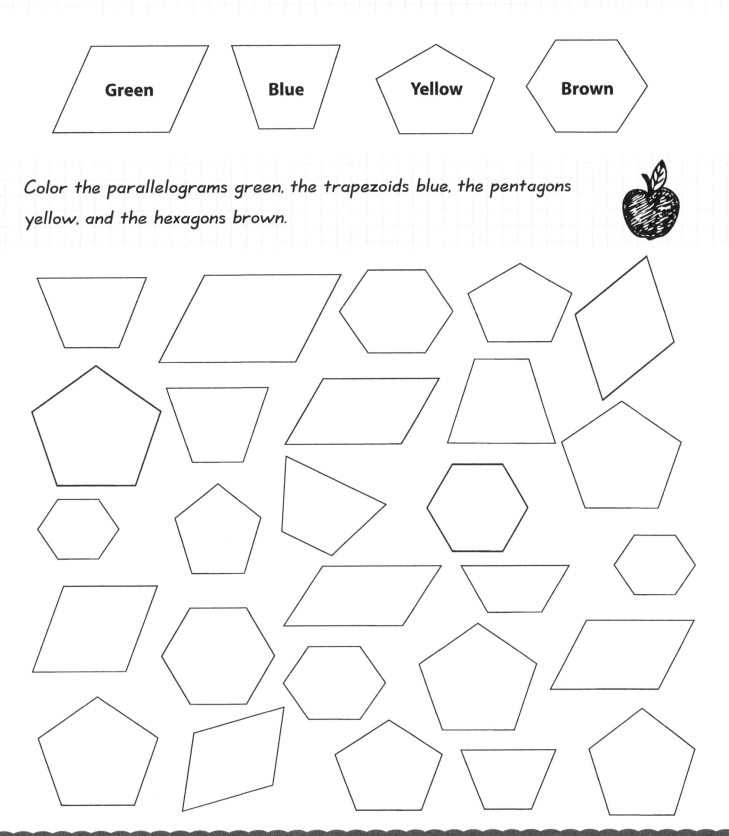

WELL DONE!
YOU KNOW ONE MORE SHAPE NOW AND CAN TAKE A LITTLE BREAK AND PLAY.

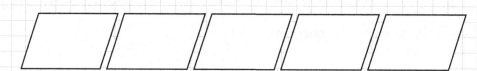

Color 2 parallelograms blue and the rest yellow.
How many parallelograms are there?

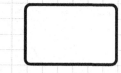 + 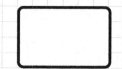 =

Blue   Yellow   Parallelograms

COLOR THE OBJECT(S) GREEN THAT ROLL

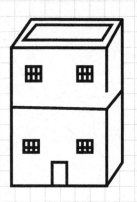

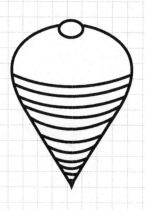

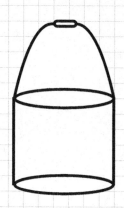

Find out who holds the heart balloon, the oval balloon, and the star balloon

TRAPEZOID

Trace the big trapezoid and color the other trapezoids.

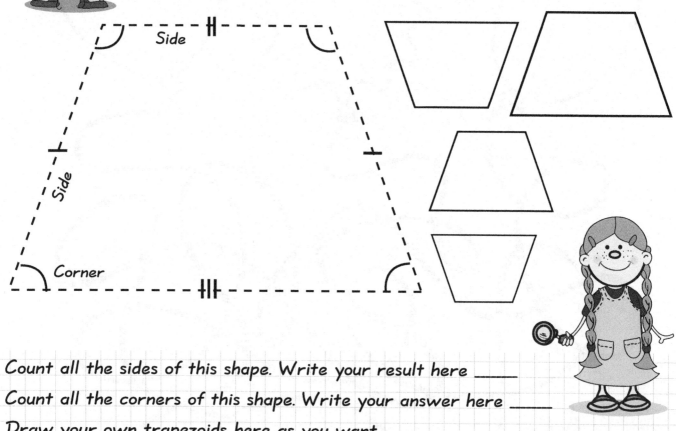

Side

Side

Corner

Count all the sides of this shape. Write your result here _____

Count all the corners of this shape. Write your answer here _____

Draw your own trapezoids here as you want...

Choose only the trapezoids from all other shapes, and color them in different colors.

How many times is each shape used? Write your answer below.

Find the trapezoids and color them in the same color.

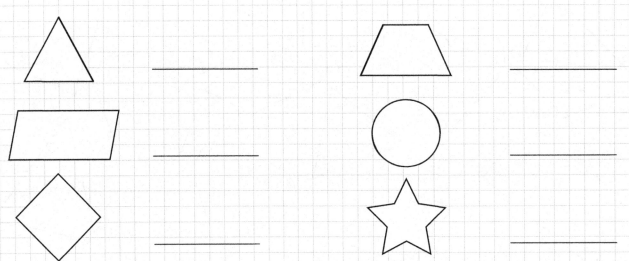

COLOR THE SHAPES

Pink   **Red**   **Blue**   **Green**

Color the squares pink, the triangles red, the parallelograms blue, and the trapezoids green.

WELL DONE!
YOU KNOW ONE MORE SHAPE NOW AND CAN TAKE A LITTLE BREAK AND PLAY.

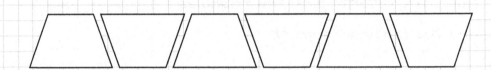

Color 4 trapezoids pink and the rest blue.

How many trapezoids are there?

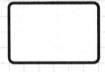 **+**  **=**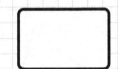

Pink   Blue   Trapezoids

COLOR THE OBJECT(S) RED THAT SLIDE

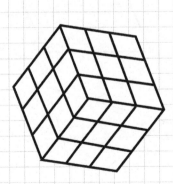

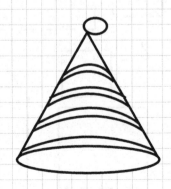

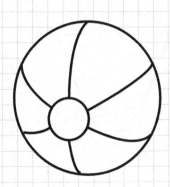

Help the boy to get a gift.

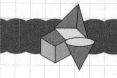

PENTAGON

Trace the big pentagon and color all other shapes.

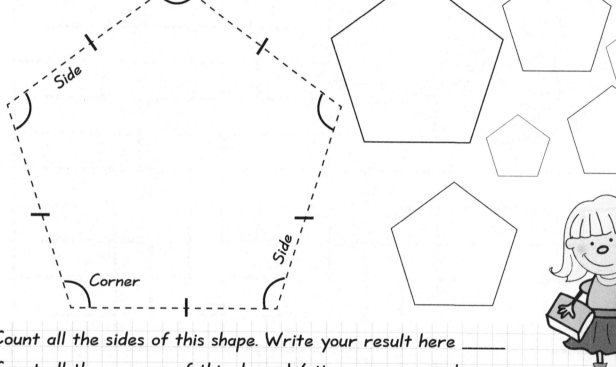

Side

Side

Side

Corner

Count all the sides of this shape. Write your result here _____

Count all the corners of this shape. Write your answer here _____

Draw your own pentagons here as you want...

Choose only the pentagons from all other shapes, and color them in different colors.

How many times is each shape used? Write your answer below.

Find the pentagons and color them in the same color.

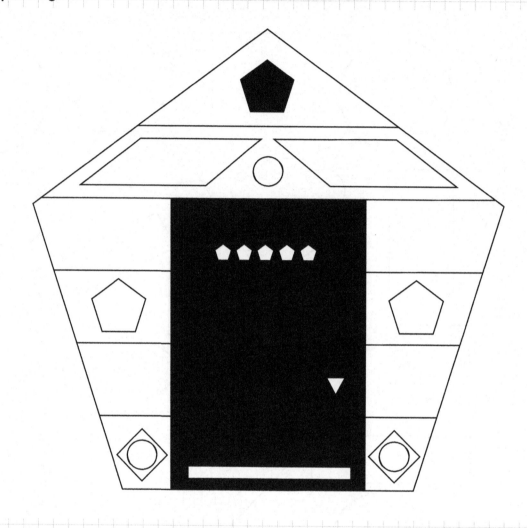

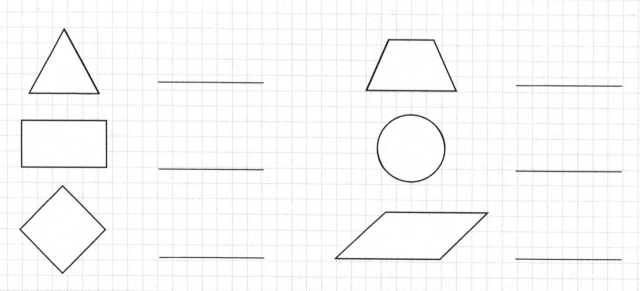

COLOR THE SHAPES

Brown **Yellow** **Green** **Blue**

Color the parallelograms brown, the trapezoid yellow,
the pentagons green, and the triangles blue.

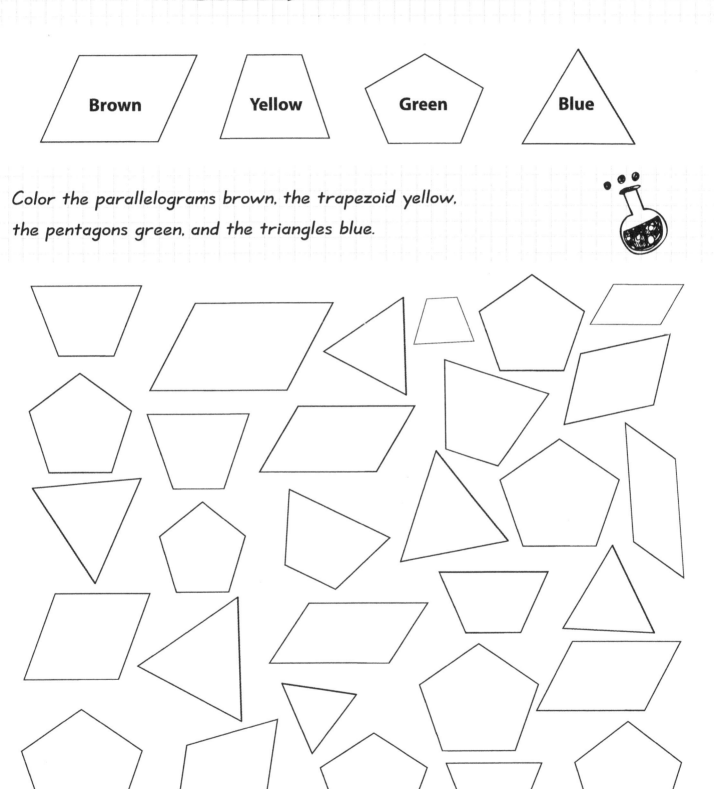

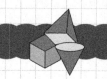

WELL DONE!
YOU KNOW ONE MORE SHAPE NOW AND CAN TAKE A LITTLE BREAK AND PLAY.

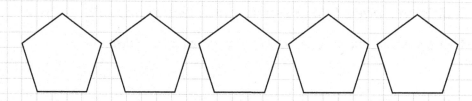

Color each second pentagon brown and the rest green. How many pentagons are there?

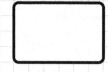 **+** 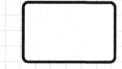 **=**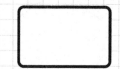

Brown   Green   Pentagons

COLOR THE OBJECT(S) BROWN THAT SLIDE AND STACK.

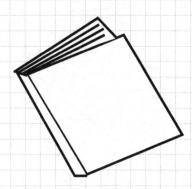

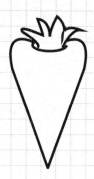

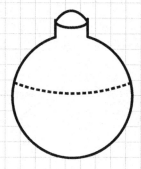

Cut out the paper and assemble the Pentagonal Prism.

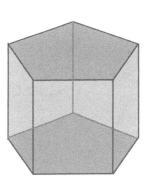

PENTAGONAL PRISM

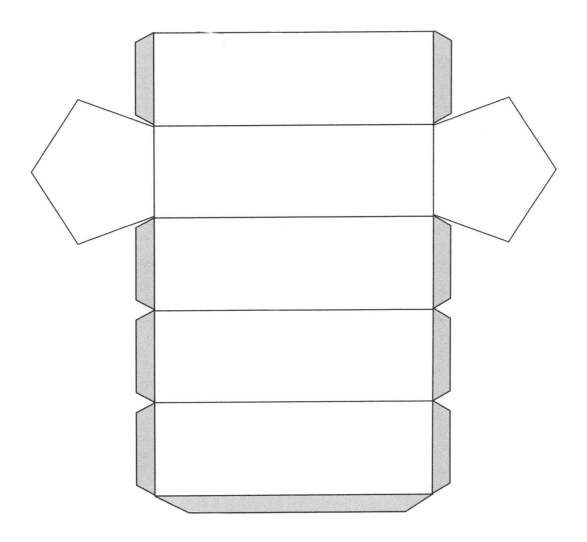

HEXAGON

Trace the big hexagon and color all other hexagons.

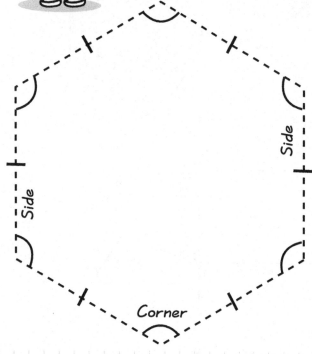

Side
Side
Side
Corner

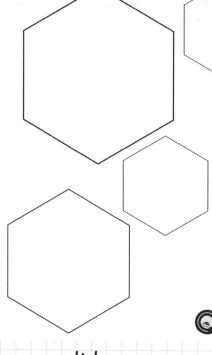

Count all the sides of this shape. Write your result here _____

Count all the corners of this shape. Write your answer here _____

Draw your own hexagons here as you want...

GEOMETRY FOR FUN!

Choose only the hexagons from all the shapes, and color them in different colors.

How many times is each shape used? Write your answer below.

Find the hexagons and color them in the same color.

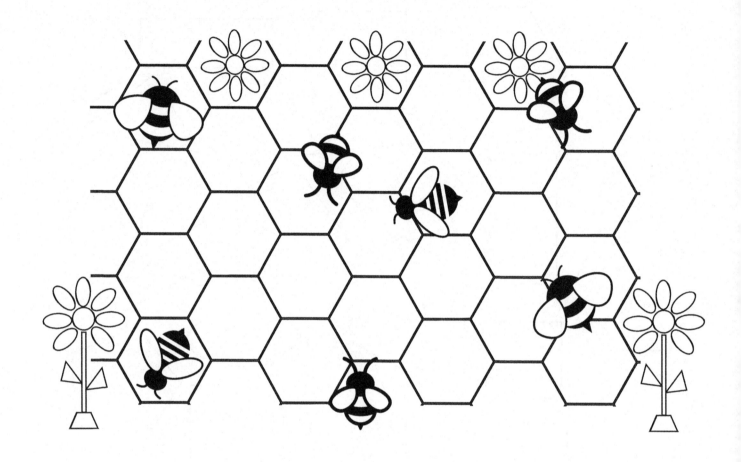

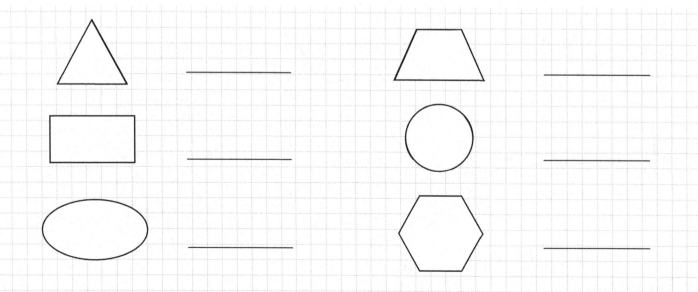

GEOMETRY FOR FUN!

COLOR THE SHAPES

Brown **Yellow** **Green** **Blue**

Color the hexagons brown, the trapezoids yellow,
the pentagons green, and the triangles blue.

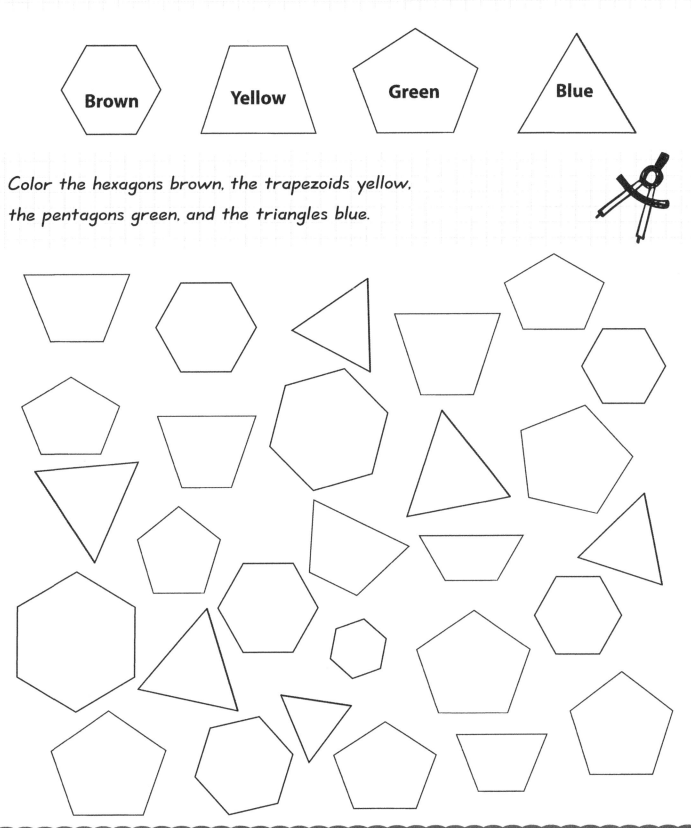

WELL DONE!
YOU KNOW ONE MORE SHAPE NOW AND CAN TAKE A LITTLE BREAK AND PLAY.

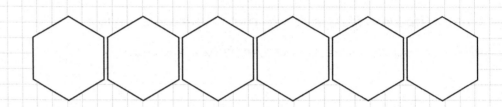

Color each second hexagon yellow and the rest orange. How many hexagons are there?

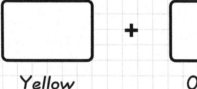

Yellow   +   Orange   =   Hexagons

COLOR THE OBJECT(S) ORANGE THAT ROLL AND STACK

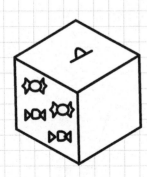

Find the hidden numbers and fill in all the empty cells at the bottom

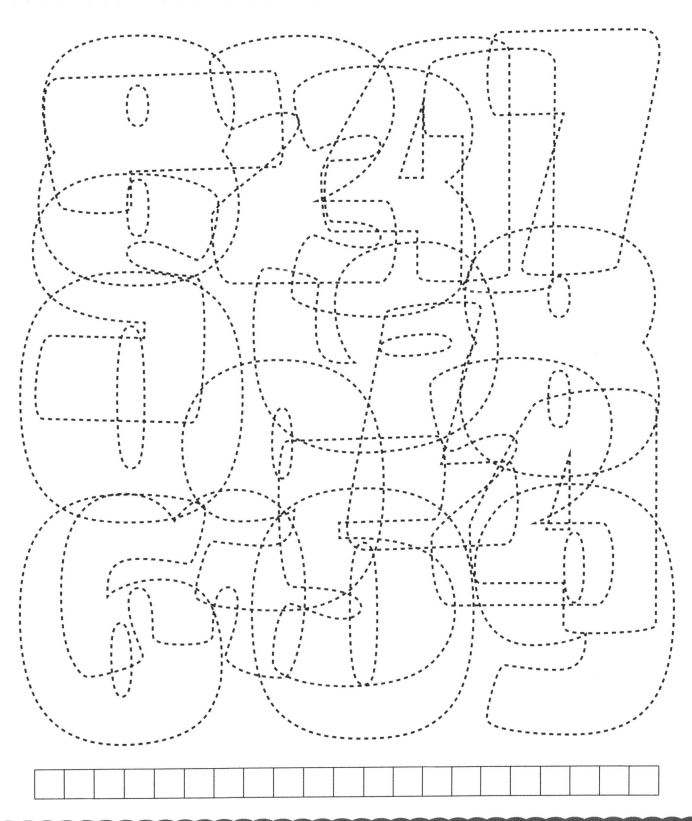

STAR

Trace the big star and color all others stars

Corner

Side

Corner

Side

Side

Count all the sides of this shape. Write your result here _____

Count all the corners of this shape. Write your answer here _____

Draw your own stars here as you want...

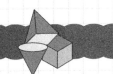

Choose only the stars from all the shapes, and color them in different colors.

How many times is each shape used? Write your answer below.

Find the stars and color them in the same color.

COLOR THE SHAPES

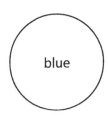 green

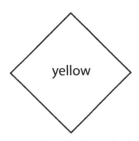 blue

yellow

brown

Color the square green, the circle blue, the diamonds yellow, and the stars brown.

WELL DONE!
YOU KNOW ONE MORE SHAPE NOW AND CAN TAKE A LITTLE BREAK AND PLAY.

Color last 3 stars yellow and the rest red.

How many stars are there?

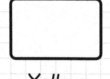 **+** 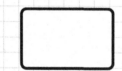 **=**

Yellow   Red   Stars

COLOR THE OBJECT(S) YELLOW THAT ROLL

Find the 6 differences

HEART

Trace the big heart and color the others hearts.

The heart doesn't have well-defined corners and sides,

so don't try to count them.

Draw your own hearts here as you want...

Choose only the hearts from all the shapes, and color them in different colors.

How many times is each shape used? Write your answer below.

Find the hearts and color them in the same color.

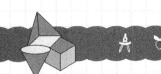

COLOR THE SHAPES

blue   green   yellow   red

Color the rectangles blue, the triangles green, the ovals yellow, and the hearts red.

2+2=4

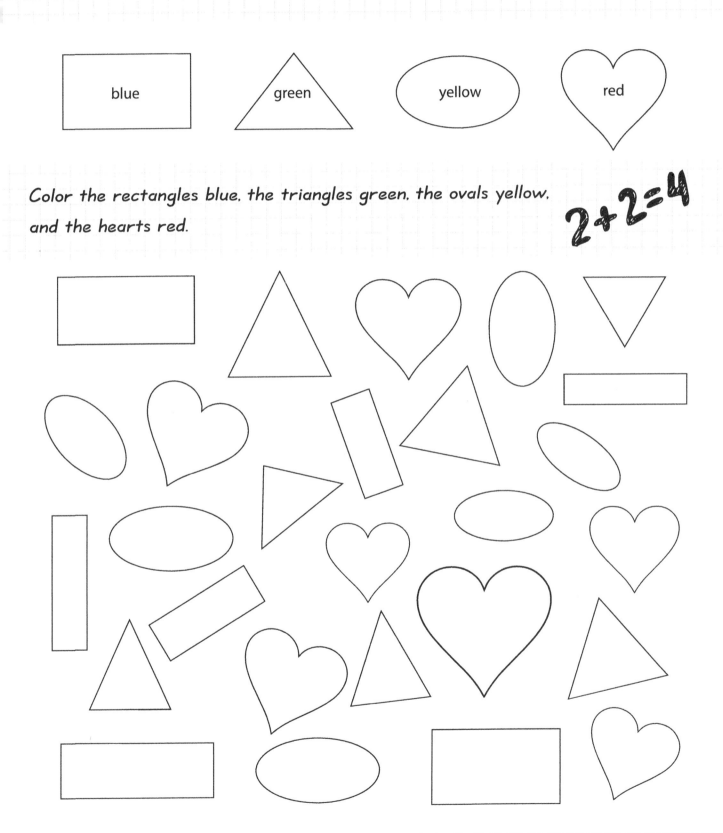

WELL DONE!
YOU KNOW ONE MORE SHAPE NOW AND CAN TAKE A LITTLE BREAK AND PLAY.

Color 4 hearts in different colors and leave the rest as it is. How many hearts are there?

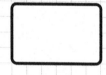 + 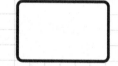 =

Colored   Colorless   Hearts

COLOR THE OBJECT(S) GREEN THAT ROLL

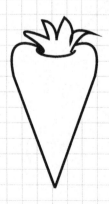

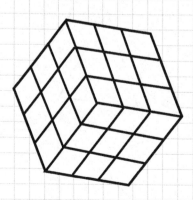

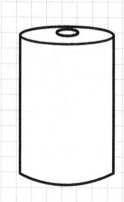

Find regularity and color the mat

So, you know all the basic geometric shapes now. You can understand their properties and ready to further travel to the world of geometry. On the way, even more exciting tasks are waiting in the 3D Shape's Kingdom. We will be happy to meet you in the next book!

FOR NOTES

_____

_____

_____

_____

_____

_____

_____

_____

_____

_____

_____

_____

_____

_____

_____

_____

_____

_____

GEOMETRY FOR FUN!

Develop your imagination

Homeschooling Workbook for kids 5-8 years old. Fun and interesting tasks, exciting activities and coloring page, introduce to your kid awesome world of Geometry

Authors:

Anna Zubrytska

Designer:

Feodor Zubrytsky

Editor:

Amanda Marlone

Copyright © 2018
Anna Zubrytska
Fun Book for Kids and
Their Parents
All Rights Reserved

In this book, we made every effort to make the first acquaintance with geometry fun, exciting, simple, and as clear as possible game for the child.

The book presents the basic elementary geometric shapes in 2D space: a circle, a square, a triangle, a rectangle, a parallelogram, a trapezoid, a pentagon, a hexagon, a star, and a heart. The main properties of each figure are presented in a fascinating form, the number of sides, corners, their differences, and similarities as well. The consolidation of the covered material is accompanied by exciting tasks, colorings, and rebuses.

We believe that acquaintance with this book will make the future study of geometry for a child easy and simple, because the book lays down the basic geometric concepts at a fairly early age and perfectly prepares the kid for more complex future tasks.

www.funbookforkids.com